RACE TO THE POLES

BY AMY C. REA

MOMENTUM

Published by The Child's World®
1980 Lookout Drive • Mankato, MN 56003-1705
800-599-READ • www.childsworld.com

ISBN 9781503832213
LCCN 2018962831

Printed in the United States of America
PA02421

ABOUT THE AUTHOR

Amy C. Rea grew up in northern Minnesota and now lives in a Minneapolis suburb with her
husband, two sons, and dog. She writes frequently about traveling around Minnesota.

CONTENTS

MOMENTUM

FAST FACTS

The First North Pole Explorers

► In the 1800s, British explorers made attempts to find the North Pole. None of them were successful. But several of them set records for getting closer and closer.

► In 1898, U.S. explorer Robert Peary made his first attempt to reach the North Pole. It was not successful.

The First South Pole Explorers

► In the 1770s, British captain James Cook documented evidence of Antarctica's existence, such as icebergs in southern waters. Although he didn't see the continent, Cook and his crew were the first people to cross the **Antarctic Circle**.

► In 1902, British navy officer and explorer Robert Scott made his first attempt to reach the South Pole. It was not successful. However, he continued his efforts to reach the pole.

► In 1908, British explorer Ernest Shackleton attempted to reach the South Pole. Although he got closer than Scott did, he was also unsuccessful.

**Temperatures in Antarctica range from ►
-76 degrees Fahrenheit (-60°C) to
14 degrees Fahrenheit (-10°C).**

CHAPTER ONE

THE RACE TO THE NORTH POLE

The wind tore at the group of men heading north. They walked through snow and ice near a churning sea. The wind was biting and cold. It hurt to breathe in the freezing, harsh air. The men had been **trekking** nearly 15 miles (24 km) per day with sleds and sled dogs. It was hard, tiring work. But it was important. They wanted to be the first people to reach the North Pole.

Their leader was U.S. explorer and doctor Frederick Cook. In February 1908, Dr. Cook and nine **Inuit** left a settlement in Greenland called Annoatok, heading for the pole. At first, the trek went well. But as the group went farther north, the wind and brutally cold temperatures made the journey more difficult. The sky had rolling gray clouds. The explorers saw only sea and ice in every direction. Dr. Cook was not exactly sure what the North Pole even looked like.

◄ **Dr. Frederick Cook faced rough weather conditions during his journey to the North Pole.**

In late April, Dr. Cook noticed a polar sea that was frozen, yet moving. Beyond it, there was a large flat-topped ice island. The ice island stood higher and thicker than the sea ice. On April 21, 1908, Dr. Cook's team arrived at the ice island. They spent two days there. Dr. Cook took many scientific notes. He used a **sextant**, which is a tool for navigation, to determine his latitude and longitude. Those measurements convinced him that they had become the first people to reach the North Pole.

The excitement at being the first people to arrive there did not last long. The return trip was difficult. Dr. Cook's team ended up going west rather than east. Winter set in. Howling winds and snowstorms made it impossible for them to see where they were going. Deep snowdrifts were difficult to walk through. They found a cave on Devon Island in Canada and camped there for four months. At first, they used rifles to hunt for meat to eat. But they eventually ran out of bullets. They had to use spears instead. They worried about being able to survive long enough to return home.

They were not able to leave Devon Island until February 1909. In April, they arrived back in Greenland. Dr. Cook telegraphed the *New York Herald* to let the world know he was the first person to arrive at the North Pole. He wanted to share his story.

Walruses are one animal that lives in the Arctic. ▶

▲ Dr. Cook and his companions stuck a U.S. flag into
— an igloo during their trek to the North Pole.

The front-page headline of the newspaper read, "The North Pole
is Discovered by Dr. Frederick A. Cook."[1]

However, a week later, the New York Times printed its own
story titled, "Peary Discovers the North Pole After Eight Trials in
23 Years."[2] The story said U.S. explorer Robert Peary was actually
the first person to arrive at the pole. Peary said only one team
had actually reached the North Pole: his own team. He claimed
that Dr. Cook had not arrived at the North Pole at all.

Dr. Cook's Route

Peary's Route

ARCTIC OCEAN

Ellesmere
Island

North
Pole

Greenland

CHAPTER TWO

WHO ARRIVED FIRST?

In 1891, Robert Peary sailed to Greenland. The ship creaked and groaned as it rose and fell with the waves. Cold gusts of wind chilled everyone on deck. Peary wanted to explore the areas north of North America. When Peary put together a crew for the expedition, he included a doctor: Frederick Cook. Dr. Cook was interested in exploring the north, too. When Peary broke two leg bones in an accident on the ship, Dr. Cook was able to set the broken bones. Peary was able to heal. He was very grateful to Dr. Cook and glad to have him along for the journey. But the two men did not always get along. Peary wanted to be the first person to see the North Pole because it could bring him fame and fortune. Dr. Cook was more interested in learning things about the area. However, they did not reach the pole during that expedition.

◄ **Robert Peary was in the U.S. Navy and explored the Arctic during his time off.**

▲ **In 2015, President Barack Obama announced that Mount McKinley's name would change to Denali, which is what Alaskan Natives have called the mountain for thousands of years.**

In 1893, Peary planned another expedition. Dr. Cook did not go. However, Dr. Cook was not done exploring the north. He traveled to Alaska to try and climb Denali, which was known at the time as Mount McKinley.

Both men continued trying to reach the North Pole. They each had their own expeditions. But it was hard to know exactly where the North Pole was. The North Pole is located in an area of drifting sea ice. Because the ice moves all the time, it is hard to find the specific spot for the North Pole without detailed scientific measurements.

On April 21, 1908, Dr. Cook was convinced he had reached the North Pole. He spent two days taking measurements and writing notes. Some of those notes were placed in a brass tube and buried in a **crevasse** to prove they had arrived. Then, Dr. Cook and his team began the return journey. They did not arrive back in Annoatok until April 1909. There, Dr. Cook learned that many people thought he was dead because he had been gone so long. He also learned that Peary had started his own North Pole expedition eight months earlier.

On April 6, 1909, a crew member told Peary that he felt they were close to the pole. Peary attached a U.S. flag to a staff. Then, he mounted it on top of an igloo. He watched it wave in the wind.

A GROUNDBREAKING EXPLORER

Matthew Henson was one of several men in Peary's crew. But unlike the other men, he was African American. At age 13, he became a cabin boy on a ship. The captain taught him to read and write. Later, Henson met Peary in Washington, DC. Peary offered him a job and Henson accompanied Peary on numerous expeditions over 20 years. He was a member of the crew that arrived at the North Pole in 1909. Henson later said, "I think I'm the first man to sit on top of the world."[3]

The next day, Peary took out his sextant and took measurements. He did not tell his crew what the results were. He took a piece of the flag and put it in a tin container along with a note and buried it in the ice. Then, they began their return journey.

At Annoatok, Dr. Cook prepared to go home. But Dr. Cook could not carry much equipment on the return journey. He met Harry Whitney, an American who was hunting in the Arctic. Whitney suggested Dr. Cook leave some equipment behind. Whitney could bring it to Dr. Cook in New York later. Dr. Cook agreed. He left behind his records and his instruments, including the sextant.

But Whitney had a problem. He had planned on taking a boat from Greenland to the United States, but it did not arrive. The first boat that came to Annoatok was Peary's. Peary offered Whitney a ride back on his boat. But Peary refused to bring Dr. Cook's possessions with them. Whitney had no choice. All of Dr. Cook's records stayed in Annoatok.

On September 21, 1909, Dr. Cook arrived in New York City. He was greeted by many people who cheered for him. Later, he met with reporters. He showed them his notebook and told them that his sextant and records would soon be in New York. He said those would prove he had discovered the North Pole.

But then he learned what Peary had done. Without proof, Peary claimed Dr. Cook was wrong. He found ways to **discredit** Dr. Cook. He found someone who claimed Dr. Cook had lied about climbing Denali. He also quoted Dr. Cook's crew members as saying they were not sure if they had reached the North Pole.

No one ever discovered the notes both Dr. Cook and Peary said they left at the North Pole. Finding those might prove one of them to be correct. But as years passed, many other explorers made their way to the North Pole. They found that Dr. Cook's descriptions were accurate. However, it is still not proven that Dr. Cook was the first person to arrive there.

A THIRD POSSIBILITY

Today, some scientists and historians believe that neither Peary nor Dr. Cook actually made it all the way to the North Pole. The very first visit might have actually happened decades later. Joseph Fletcher was in the U.S. Air Force and landed a ski-modified jet at the North Pole on May 3, 1952. Fletcher left the jet and walked to the exact location of the North Pole. He may truly be the first person to have done so.

CHAPTER THREE

THE RACE TO THE SOUTH POLE

In June 1910, Norwegian explorer Roald Amundsen and his crew set sail from Norway. He had his sight set on becoming the first person to reach the South Pole. When the group arrived in Antarctica, it was like seeing an entirely new world. Everything was white and gray. The wind was bitterly cold. They unloaded their sleds and gear from the ship and began the long, physically demanding trek.

On December 14, 1911, Amundsen and his crew of four men were thrilled. They had spent nearly two months journeying across the frozen Antarctic. But that day, their instruments showed they had reached the South Pole. They were the first people ever to arrive there. Amundsen planted flags in the snow to prove he had been there. He and his team spent a few days taking scientific measurements.

◄ **Roald Amundsen (left) wanted to visit the North Pole. But when he heard someone had already made it there, he decided to go the South Pole instead.**

▲ **Four other men joined Scott on his expedition to the South Pole. Left to right are Lawrence Oates, Henry Bowers, Scott, Edward Wilson, and Edgar Evans.**

The same month Amundsen left Norway, explorer Robert Scott and his crew left Wales, a country in the United Kingdom. They were also aiming to reach the South Pole first. Scott was excited and felt confident in his journey.

The adventure proved to be very difficult. The weather was terrible. In Antarctica, storms left behind deep snows for the explorers to travel through. The cold was bitter and the wind was harsh. By the end of December, most of the crew left the expedition. Only five men pushed forward through the brutal winter weather.

▲ Scott and his team arrived in Antarctica
in the *Terra Nova*.

On January 17, 1912, the men arrived at the South Pole. It should have been a thrilling time. But when they arrived, they saw the flags that Amundsen left. They knew that meant Scott's team was not the first to find the South Pole. Their hard work and horrible travel conditions had been for nothing. They were not the first.

Scott was very disappointed. He turned his small crew around and began the return journey. The weather got even worse. At times, they were forced to stay in their tent for days because blizzards made it impossible to travel. At one point, they were only 11 miles (18 km) from their base camp. But the weather forced them to stay in one place. They did not have enough food and fuel to use during this time. They grew weaker and weaker. By spring 1912, all five explorers had died.

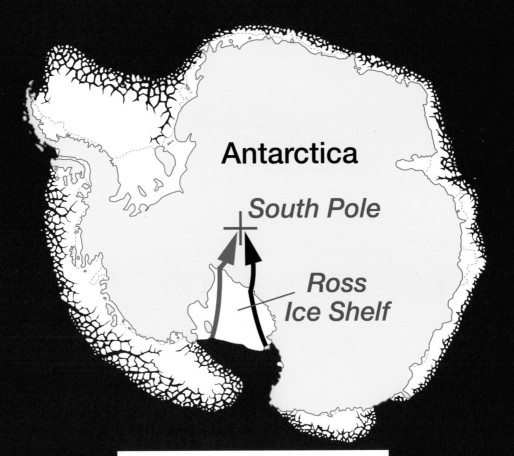

Antarctica

South Pole

Ross
Ice Shelf

Amundsen's Route →
Scott's Route →

CHAPTER FOUR

FACTORS IN THE SOUTH POLE RACE

Amundsen's crew got the sled dogs lined up and attached to the sleds. The dogs were barking, but they were well trained and ready to do their job. Amundsen gave the order, and the dogs leapt into action, pulling sleds carrying food and gear.

Both Amundsen and Scott wanted to be the first person to reach the South Pole. One succeeded and returned home, safe and a hero. One arrived at the South Pole a month later. He and many members of his team died before they could return home. There were many factors that affected both Amundsen and Scott in their quests to reach the South Pole.

During Amundsen's travels in the Arctic, he learned how to use sled dogs. Inuit taught him how valuable sled dogs could be. They could pull heavy loads while also traveling quickly.

◄ **Sled dogs helped Amundsen's team travel more than 20 miles (32 km) each day.**

Amundsen had much experience with them and knew how to use them.

Scott brought sled dogs, too. He also brought motor sleds and ponies. But the motor sleds were not reliable. And the ponies had special snow shoes, but they were so heavy that even with snow shoes they sank in the soft snow. Nobody on Scott's crew had much experience with sled dogs. They did not know the best ways to work with them.

Another way explorers could get around Antarctica was with skis. Both men brought skis for themselves and their crews. Amundsen and his crew were from Norway. Skis were often used for transportation there. He and his crew knew how to use them. They strapped them on and raced across the snow. The skis helped propel them over snowy areas that would be difficult to hike through. Knowing how to ski made this easier. Scott and most of his crew did not know how to ski. Scott brought along an expert skier to teach them, but the crew had trouble learning.

Dressing appropriately was also important for the journey to the South Pole. Amundsen learned about dressing warmly and safely from Inuit. They used clothing made of furs. They did not allow the furs to fit tightly. That allowed any sweat to run off and **evaporate**. If the furs were tight, the sweat could freeze. That could lead to **hypothermia**.

Scott's crew, on the other hand, used woolen underwear. They wore windproof outer layers over the wool. Layering clothes is usually a good idea in cold places. But in Antarctica, layering allowed the sweat to freeze into ice under their clothes.

One of the biggest factors was something neither explorer had control over: the weather. Amundsen had better timing. He arrived in the Antarctic earlier than Scott. The weather during Amundsen's journey was much better. Amundsen and his crew left the South Pole just as unusually severe winter weather started. Because they arrived later, Scott and his crew trekked into terrible blizzards and bitterly cold temperatures. Scott and his crew faced weather extremes that Amundsen luckily avoided.

HONORING BOTH EXPLORERS

Although Amundsen won the race to the South Pole, Scott's efforts were not forgotten. In 2008, the National Science Foundation opened a new research station at the South Pole. It was named the Amundsen-Scott South Pole Station. The new station can hold more than 100 people. It has modern research and living facilities. Scientists there can continue studying the wonders of the Antarctic while remembering the explorers who first arrived there.

▲ Scott did his best to dress warmly for
the freezing temperatures.

Polar exploration can be very dangerous. Planning ahead provided protection for some explorers. But timing and luck also played a part in Amundsen's and Scott's journeys. In the end, Amundsen was first seen as the hero because he won the race. The public was as interested in the discovery of the South Pole as it had been by the discovery of the North Pole. But the tragic deaths of Scott and his crew caught the public's attention. Scott was also seen as a hero, even though he had been unsuccessful. When Scott's final letters and diaries were found by later explorers, it earned more attention than Amundsen's success.

THINK ABOUT IT

► Would you like to have been the first person to travel to either the North or South Pole? Why or why not?
► Who do you think arrived at the North Pole first? Do some more research on the topic and explain your answer.
► Do you think it's important for people to explore places that humans have never visited? Why or why not?

GLOSSARY

Antarctic Circle (ant-AHRK-tik SUR-kuhl): The Antarctic Circle is an imaginary line around Earth that is north of the South Pole. Explorers crossed the Antarctic Circle.

crevasse (kruh-VAS): A crevasse is a break or a deep crack in ice. Dr. Cook buried his notes in a crevasse.

discredit (diss-CRED-it): To discredit something is to make people believe that thing is not true. Peary tried to discredit Dr. Cook's claims about reaching the North Pole.

evaporate (i-VAP-uh-rate): Evaporate means to change to a gas or vapor. The sweat did not evaporate.

hypothermia (hipe-oh-THUR-mee-uh): Hypothermia happens when the human body becomes too cold. North and South Pole explorers were in danger of hypothermia.

Inuit (IN-yoo-it): Inuit are a Native group in Greenland, northern Alaska, and arctic Canada. Inuit taught explorers how to survive in cold temperatures.

sextant (SEK-stunt): A sextant is a scientific tool that measures angular distances to discover what latitude and longitude one is at. Dr. Cook used a sextant to find out if he had reached the North Pole.

trekking (TREK-king): Trekking is a type of travel that is usually slow and difficult, and may involve hauling items along. Dr. Cook's team was trekking toward the North Pole.

SOURCE NOTES

1. Bruce Henderson. "Who Discovered the North Pole?" *Smithsonian.com*. Smithsonian, Apr. 2009. Web. 26 Dec. 2018.

2. Ibid.

3. Brian Clark Howard. "Historic Photos Celebrate Pioneering Black Explorer." *National Geographic*. National Geographic Society, 13 Feb. 2018. Web. 26 Dec. 2018.

TO LEARN MORE

BOOKS

Gifford, Clive. *Polar Lands.* New York, NY: Kingfisher, 2017.

Morlock, Rachael. *Roald Amundsen Reaches the South Pole.* New York, NY: PowerKids Press, 2019.

Roxburgh, Ellis. *Robert Peary vs. Frederick Cook: Race to the North Pole.* New York, NY: Gareth Stevens Publishing, 2016.

WEBSITES

Visit our website for links about the North and South Poles:
childsworld.com/links

Note to Parents, Teachers, and Librarians: We routinely verify our Web links to make sure they are safe and active sites. So encourage your readers to check them out!

INDEX